Rules Help

Marvin Buckley

Put away
your things.

Rules help me know what to do
at school.

Swings
for
Toddlers
Only

Rules help me know what to do
at the playground.

3

Rules help me know what to do at the park.

Rules help me know what to do at the library.

Do Not Run
Near the Pool

Rules help me know what to do
at the pool.

Wear bowling shoes.

Rules help me know what to do at the bowling alley.

Rules help me know what to do at home.